M000074648

The Kazakh Phrasebook

Aijan Akhmetova

Contents

1. Most common expressions

Hello!	Salemetsiz be/Amansiz ba
Yes (formal)	Ia
Yes/Yeah (informal)	Aha
I can't speak Kazakh well	Men kazaksha onsha emes bilemin
Maybe	Mumkin
No, thank you	Jok, rahmet
I'm sorry	Keshiriniz
Excuse me	Keshiriniz
Please	Otinemin
How much do you want for this?	Bul ushin kansha suraisiz?
Excuse me, where is the restroom?	Keshiriniz, darethana kaida?
Do you understand English?	Siz agylshynsha tusinesiz be?
Do you speak English?	Siz agylshynsha bilesiz be?
Excuse me	Keshiriniz
Just a minute	Kazir

That's alright	Eshtene etpeidi/Bari jaksi
What did you say?	Ne aittiniz?
It doesn't matter	Eshteme emes
I don't speak Kazakh	Men kazaksha bilmeimin
I speak only a little Kazakh	Men kazaksha tek kishkene bilemin
I don't understand Kazakh	Men kazaksha tusinbeimin
I understand only a little Kazakh	Men kazaksha tek kishkene tusinemin
I'm sorry, could you repeat that?	Keshiriniz, osini kaitalap jiberesiz be?
How do you say … in Kazakh?	…kazaksha kalai aitiladi?
What does that mean?	Bul neni bildiredi?
Please, repeat	Kaitalap jiberinizshi

2. At the Airport

Passport	Pasport
Ticket	Bilet
Where did you arrive from?	Kaidan kelesiz?
Where are you traveling?	Kaida sapar shektiniz?
How many bags do you have?	Kansha sumkaniz bar ?

4. Introductions

My name is John	Menin atim Djon
What is your name?	Sizdin atiniz kalay?
Nice to meet you	Kezdeskenimizge kuanishtimin
How are you?	Kalaisiz?
Good/ very good	Jaksi/ote jaksi
And you	Siz she?
Alright	Jaksi
So-so	Onsha emes/jai
Bad	Jaman
Bye	Sau bol
Goodbye	Sau boliniz
This is my…	Bul menin…
… wife	…ayelim
…boyfriend	… jigitim
…girlfriend	… kizim

4

…son	…ulim
…daughter	…kizim/kiz balam
I work for	Men...jumis isteimin
I'm here…	Men osinda…
…on vacation	…dem aluga toktadim
…for work	…jumispen
…from United States	…Amerikadan keldim/…Kurama shtattarinan keldim
I am married	Men turmistamin
I am single	Men boidakpin
Yes	Ia
I understand	Men tusinemin
Not	…emes.
Do you understand	Tusinesiz be?
Excuse me/Sorry	Keshiriniz
I'm an American	Men Amerikandikpin

I live in…	Men...turamin
I speak English	Men agylshynsha bilemin
Do you speak English?	Agylshynsha bilesiz be?
I speak Kazakh	Men kazaksha bilemin
A little	Kishkene
Do you speak Kazakh	Siz kazaksha bilesiz be?
Pleasure to do business with you	Sizben jumis isteuge kuanishtimin
I have an appointment with	Magan…kezdesu uakiti belgilengen
Here is my business card	Menin vizitkam osi
I work for	Men...jumis isteimin
Do you want?	Tileisiz be?
I want…	Men…keledi
I don't want…	Men...kelmeidi
…to eat	…jeuge…
…to drink	…ishuge…

6

I want to go…	Men…bargim keledi
I don't want to go…	Men…batgim kelmeidi
…to the restaurant	…restoranga…
…to the hotel	…otelgb…/…konak uige…
…to a concert	…konsertke…/…sauik keshine…
…home	…uige…
…to the movies	…kinoga…
…for a walk	…dalaga…

Thank you	Rahmet
Please/You're welcome	Otinemin/Marhabat

4. Directions

General directions

To the left	Solga
To the right	Onga
Straight	Tuzu
Back	Keri
Take the first left/right	Solga/onga birden bur
Near the building	Gimarattin kasinda
Far	Alis
Not far	Alis emes
By foot	Jaiau
By car	Kolikpen
On the bus	Avtobuspen
How do I get to	Men…kalai bara alamin?
… Tbilisi?	…Tbilisi kalasina…
… the airport	…aeroporka…
… the hotel?	…otelge…/…konak uigb…

8

... the movie theater?	...kinoteatr**ga**...
... the museum?	...muzeug**e**.../...murajaig**a**...
... the restaurant?	...restorang**a**...
... the café?	...kafeg**e**...
... the mall?	...magazing**e**.../...saud**a** uig**e**...
... the gas station?	...benz**i**n kui**a**tin jerg**e**...
... the bazaar?	...bazarg**a**...
... the restroom?	...tualetk**e**.../...darethanag**a**...
...the train station?	...vokzalg**a**.../...auejaig**a**...
... the street?	...koshe**ge**...

Is there...	Bund**a**...bar ma?
...a bank?	...bank...
...a bus stop ?	...aialdam**a**...
...a café?	...kaf**e**...
...a store?	...magaz**i**n.../...duk**e**n...
...a church?	...shirk**e**u...

9

…a cinema?	…kinoteatr…
…a currency exchange?	…valuta airbastau punkti…
…a drugstore?	…apteka…/…darihana…
…a dry cleaners?	…kiim tazalau jer…
…a gas station?	…benzin kuiatin jer…
…a hospital?	…emhana…/auruhana…
… a parking lot?	…avtoturak…
… a restroom?	…tualet…/…darethana…

5. At the hotel

Hi, I have a reservation	Salem, men bolmege tapsiris berdim
My name is…	Menin atim…
I need a room, please	Magan bolme kerek
We need two rooms please…	Magan eki bolme…kerek
… with one bed	…bir orindi…
… with two beds	…eki orindi…
It's for…	Bul…
… a few days	…birneshe kunge
… a week	…bir aptaga
… two weeks	…eki aptaga
Is breakfast included?	Tanertengi as kosa eseptelengen be?
What time is breakfast served?	Tanertengi as neshede boladi?
Could I look at the rooms?	Bolmeni karap shiguga bola ma?
What time do I have to vacate the room?	Bolmeni bosatuga kansha uakit bar?
Could I reserve a room, please?	Bolmeni tapsiriska aluga bola ma?

Likely answers:

Yes	**Ia**
No	Jok
We don't have available rooms	Bizde bos bolme jok
No, thank you	Jok rahmet
I need...	Magan...kajet
...another blanket	...baska korpe...
...another pillow	...baska jastik...
...another towel	...baska oramal...
...more soap	...sabin...
...a razor	...ustara.../...britva...
...a hair dryer	...fen...
Please, some more...	...tagi da kosinizshi
...tea	Shai...
...coffee	Kofe...
...water	Su...

...juice	Sok...
...milk	Sut...
...bread	Nan...
...eggs	Jumirtka...

Come in	Kiriniz
Later, please	Keinirek/Sosin
I need a taxi, please	Magan taksi kajet

6. Medical issues

Major Issues

I need …	Magan…kajet
… a doctor	…dariger…
… a hospital	…emhana…
My head hurts	Menin basim auiradi
My stomach hurts	Menin ishim auirbdi
My arm hurts	Menin iigim auiradi
My hand hurts	Menin kolim auiradi
My leg hurts	Menin ayagim auiradi
My foot hurts	Menin tabanim auiradi
My back hurts	Menin arkam auiradi
My ear hurts	Menin kulagim auiradi
My kidney hurts	Menin buiregim auiradi
My neck hurts	Menbn moiinim auiradi
My throat hurts	Menin tamagim auiradi

14

It hurts right here	Mina jerde auiradi
The pain is sharp	Auru ote katti
The pain is not sharp	Auru katti emes
It hurts sometimes	Keide auiradi
It hurts all the time	Unemi auiradi

I lost…	Men…jogalttim
…my glasses	…kozildirigimdi…
…my contact lenses	…kontakt linzalardi…
…my prescription medication	…dari kagazimdi…
I have a cold	Magan suik tidi

I need some aspirin	Magan aspirin kajet
I have a fever	Kizuim koterildi
I feel dizzy	Basim ainalip jatir
I have a…	Mende…
High blood pressure	…jogari kan kisimi

15

Asthma	...**a**stma
Diabetes	...diab**et**

7. Shopping

Hello/Hi	Salemetsiz be/Salem
I need help, please	Magan komektesinizshi
I'm just looking.	Men jai karap jatirmin
Yes, please	Ia
No, thank you.	Jok, rahmet
Could I try this on please?	Osini kiip koruge bola ma?
How much does this cost?	Bul kansha turadi?
I like this	Bul magan unaidi
I don't like this	Bul magan unamaidi
That's too expensive	Bul ote kimbat
Could you lower the price?	Bagani tusiresiz be?
Is this on sale?	Bul satila ma?
I'll take this	Men minani alamin

Clothes

I need to buy...	Magan…satip alu kajet
…a belt	…belbeu…
…a bathing suit	…shomilu kostumi…
… a coat	…palto…
… a tie	…galstuk…
… a bra	…lifchik…
…panties	…shalbar…
…a sweater	…sviter…
…a shirt	…koilek…
…a jacket	…jaket…
… socks	…noski…
…pants	…dambal…
…jeans	…jinsi…
… briefs	…shorti…/kiska dambal
…boxers	…bokser…
…gloves	…kolgap…

…shoes	…ayak kiim…
…a skirt	…iubka…
… a hat	…bas kiim…
…a jacket	…jaket…

Do you have this in...	Sizde bul...tusti bar ma?
…black	…kara…
…blue	…kok…
…brown	…konir…
…green	…jasil…
…gray	…sur…
…pink	…kizgilt…
…red	…kizil…
…white	…ak…
…yellow	…sari…

Payment

Do you take…	…kabildaisiz ba?
…credit cards?	Tolem kartochkalardi…
…cash?	Kol akshani…
…dollars?	Dollarmen…
…checks?	Chekterdi…

Likely responses

Can I help you?	Sizge komek kajet pe?
Do you need anything else?	Tagi birdeme alasiz ba?
What would you like?	Ne kalaisiz?
Yes, of course	Ia, arine
No, I'm sorry	Jok, okinishti

Disputes

This is a mistake	Bul katelik

20

Food

Hello	Salemetsiz be
Where is the supermarket?	Supermarket kai jerde?
Where is the store?	Magazin kai jerde?
I need some help	Magan komek kerek
I'd like to buy	Men satip aluga kalaimin
Where is the…	…kai jerde?
Bread	Nan
Eggs	Jumirtka
Butter	Mai
Sour cream	Kaimak
Rice	Kurish
½ kilos	Jarti kilogram
¾ kilos	Tortten ush kilogram
1 kilo	Bir kilogram
2 kilos	Eki kilogram

3 kilos	Ush kilogram
4 kilos	Tort kilogram
Meat	Et
Beef	Siir eti
Pork	Shoshka eti
Chicken	Tauik
Lamb	Kozi eti
Mutton	Koi eti
Veal	Buzau eti
Shrimp	Krevetka/Azshayan
Fish	Balik
Salmon	Arkan balik
Sturgeon	Mekire/Bekire
Cod	Nalim

Fruit

Strawberry	Buldirgen/Kulpinai
Apple	Alma
Apricot	Orik
Banana	Banan
Cherry	Shie
Grapefruit	Greipfrut
A melon	Kauin
Pear	Almbrt
Pineapple	Ananas
Grapes	Juzim
Strawberry	Buldirgbn/Kulpinai
Raspberry	Tankurai

Vegetables

Carrots	Sabiz
Cabbage	Kapusta

Eggplant	Kadi
Mushrooms	Saniraukulak
Peas	Burshak/Asburshak
Green peppers	Jasil burish
Red peppers	Kizil burish
Potatoes	Kartop

Drinks

Wine	Sharap
Beer	Sira
Vodka	Arak
Whiskey	Viski
Cognac	Koniak
Milk	Sut
Mineral water	Mineral sui
Juice	Sok

Tea	Shai
Deserts	Desert
Chocolate	Shokolad
Cake	Balish
Ice cream	Balmuzdak

Condiments

Where is...	...kaida?
...the sugar?	Kant/Sheker
...the salt?	Tuz
...the tea?	Shai
...the ketchup?	Ketchup
...the sour cream?	Kaimak
...the mayonnaise?	Maionez
...the vinegar?	Sirke sui

Electronics

Hello	Salemetsiz be
I need to buy…	Magan…satip alu kajet
…batteries	…batareia…
…a camera	…kamera…
…CD player	…sidi pleier…
…headphones	…naushnik…

Smoking items

Hi, I need…	Salem, magan…
…a pack of cigarettes	…shilim…
…two packs, please	…eki korap berinizshi
…three packs	…ush korap
…a lighter	…jenilin/jenildeu
…some matches	…sirinke

Shopping for drugs

Where is the pharmacy?	Darihana kaida ornalaskan?

Hi, I need...	Salem, magan...
...some aspirin	...aspirin
...a bandage	...bint/orama
...some antiseptic	...shiritpeu dari
...insect repellent	...masaga karsi em
...lip balm	...erin dalabin/gigienichka

I need medication for...	Magan...karsi dari kajet
...bites	...shagularga
...cold	...suik tiuge
...headache	...,bas auruina
...flu	...tumauga
...sunburn	...kun kiuine

Do you have...	Sizde...bar ma?
...deodorant?	...dezodorant...

…shaving crème?	…kirinu kremi…
…razors?	…kirinu stanogi…
…some soap?	…sabin…
…some sunscreen?	…kunnen saktalu kremi…
…some tampons?	…tampondar…
…some toilet paper?	…darethana kagazi…
…some toothpaste?	…tis pastasi…
…some mouthwash?	…auiz shaiu suigi…

Miscellaneous Items

I need…	Magan…kajet
…a pen	…kalam…
…a guidebook	…jolsilteme…
…a bag	…sumka…
…a map	…karta…
…a postcard	…ashik hat…/…poshta kartochkasi…
…some paper	…kagaz …

...fork	...shanishk**i**...
...knife	...pish**a**k...
...a flashlight	...fon**ar**...

8. At the restaurant

Hello	Salemetsiz be
I need a table please	Magan ustel kajet
I need a table…	Magan ustel…kajet
… for two	…eki adamga…
… for three	…ush adamga…
… for four	…tort adamga…
Can we sit outside?	Bizge tiska otiruga bola ma?
I'd like to see the menu, please	Mazirinizdi karauga kalaimin
Can we sit inside, please	Biz ishinde otiraikshi
I have a reservation	Men ustelge tapsiris jasadim
I'd like to make a reservation	Ustelge tapsiris beruge kalaimin
Do you have an English menu?	Agylshynsha mazir bar ma?

Drinks

Could you bring me the wine list?   Sharap tizimin akelinizshi?

Could I have some...	...bola ma?
...wine?	Sharap...
...beer?	Sira...
...vodka?	Arak...
...whiskey ?	Viski ...
...cognac?	Koniak...
...milk?	Sut...
...mineral water?	Mineral suin...
...orange juice?	Apelsin sogin...
...grapefruit juice?	Greifrut sogin...
...apple juice?	Alma sogin...
...tea?	Shai...

I'd like a glass of...	Men bir stakan...kalaymin
...red wine	...kizil sharabin...
...white wine	...ak sharabin...

...champagne	...shampan...
I'd like a bottle of...	Men bir botelke...kalaymin
...red wine	...kizil sharabin...
...white wine	...ak sharabin...
...champagne	...shampan...

Other drinks

Beer	Sira
Vodka	Arak
Whiskey	Viski
Cognac	Koniak
Milk	Sut
Mineral water	Mineral sui
Juice	Sok
Tea	Shai

I'd like some…	Men…kalaymin
…soup	…sorpani…
…salad	…salatti…

Deserts

Cake	Balish
Chocolate	Shokolad
Ice cream	Balmuzdak

General food categories

Meat	Et
Beef	Siir eti
Pork	Shoshka eti
Chicken	Tauik
Lamb	Kozi eti

Mutton	Koi eti
Veal	Buzau eti
Shrimp	Krevetka/Azshayan
Fish	Balik
Salmon	Arkan balik
Sturgeon	Mekire/Bekire
Cod	Nalim

9. Entertainment

Is there a nightclub nearby?	Jakinda tungi klub bar ma?
Where is the museum?	Murajai kai jerde?
Where is the nightclub?	Tungi klub kai jerde?
Where is the theater?	Teatr kai jerde?
Where is the zoo? kai jerde?	Haiuanat bagi kai jerde?/Zoopark
Where is the swimming pool?	Juzu basseini kai jerde?

10. Problems

Police	Policia
I have a complaint narazilik bar	Mende shagim bar/Mende

Lost items

I have lost...	Men...jogalttim
...my passport	...paspotimdi
...my documents	...documentterimdi
...my ticket	...biletimdi
...my wallet	...amiyanimdi/...bumajnigimdi
...my bag	...sumkamdi
...my clothes	...kiimimdi
...my glasses	...kozildirigimdi

Defective items	
I bought this recently...	Men buni juirda...satip aldim

…at the store	…magazind**e**…/…dukend**e**…
…at the bazaar	…bazaard**a**…
This item is defective	Bul bui**i**m jarams**i**z
I have the receipt	Mend**e** kvit**a**nciya bar
I don't have the receipt	Mend**e** kvit**a**nciya jok
I need a refund	Mag**a**n ker**i** kaitar**u** kaj**e**t
I want to exchange the item	Bul buiimd**i** almastirg**i**m kel**e**di
I need to see the manager	Mag**a**n menedjerd**i** korug**e** kaj**e**t

11. Changing money

Bank	Bank
Money exchange	Aksha airbastau
Where can I exchange money?	Aksha airbastauga kaida boladi?
What is the exchange rate?	Valuta kursi kansha?
I need to exchange this please	Magan minani airbastauga kajet
I need to cash this check	Magan chek akshasin alu kajet
Here is…	Mine/Minau/Mineki
…my passport	…menin paspotim

12. General Reference Information

When	Kashan
Right now	Dal kazir
Later	Sosin/Keinirek/Kein
Not right now	Kazir emes
Maybe	Mumkin
Where	Kaida
Here	Bunda/Osinda/Osi jerde
There	Sonda/Onda/Anda
Far/Not far	Alis/Alis emes
Good	Jaksi
Bad	Jaman
Expensive	Kimbat
Cheap	Arzan
What time is it?	Sagat kansha?
How much?	Kansha?/Neshe?

One	Bir
Two	Eki
Three	Ush
Four	Tort
Five	Bes
Six	Alti
Seven	Jeti
Eight	Segiz
Nine	Togiz
Ten	On
Eleven	On bir
Twelve	On eki
Thirteen	On ush
Fourteen	On tort
Fifteen	On bes
Sixteen	On alti

Seventeen	On jet**i**
Eighteen	On seg**iz**
Nineteen	On tog**iz**
Twenty	Jiirm**a**
Thirty	Ot**iz**
Forty	Kir**i**k
Fifty	El**u**
Sixty	Alp**is**
Seventy	Jetp**is**
Eighty	Seks**e**n
Ninety	Toks**a**n
One hundred	Juz
Two hundred	Ek**i** juz
Three hundred	Ush juz
Four hundred	Tort juz
Five hundred	Bes juz

Six hundred	Alt**i** juz
Seven hundred	Jet**i** juz
Eight hundred	Seg**iz** juz
Nine hundred	Tog**iz** juz
One thousand	Min
Two thousand	Ek**i** min
I have	Mend**e** bar
You have	Send**e** bar

Made in the USA
Middletown, DE
17 March 2017